IT'S NOT YOUR FAULT

WALKING BY FAITH NOT FEAR

VOL. 1

RACHELLE CHERRY

Copyright © 2021 by Rachelle Cherry

All rights reserved. No part of this publication may be reproduced, distributed, or transmitted in any form or by any means, including photocopying, recording, or other electronic or mechanical methods, without the prior written permission of the publisher, except in the case of brief quotations embodied in critical reviews and certain other noncommercial uses permitted by copyright law. For permission requests, write to the publisher, and Author addressed "Attention: Permissions Coordinator" at the address below

Printed in the United States of American

First printing, 2021

ISBN: 978-0-578-99091-0

Email: itsnotyourfault.pub@gmail.com

Contents

Acknowledgments iv

Dedication vi

Introduction viii

Denial & Depression 1

Fear 23

Frustration 28

Anger 30

Grief & Sorrow 34

Acceptance 36

Healing 40

Advocacy 47

Daily Confessions 54

Acknowledgments

I would like to honor my Lord and Savior Jesus Christ for helping me through one of the hardest fights in my life. I'm thankful for His grace to share my revelation about a parent's love for their child with special needs. His love gave me strength and the freedom of knowing that God will fulfill every promise.

I am thankful for my husband Craig Cherry and our children Aniyah and Craig D. Cherry for their love and encouragement.

I would like to thank my leaders Apostle Travis Jennings and Pastor Stephanie Jennings for their consistency, love, and support for my family and my spiritual growth.

A special thanks to Pamela Tucker who helped me through the writing journey and provided support.

Last but not the least, I would like to thank my family and church community for always believing in me and giving me the support needed to persevere.

Dedication

---- ★★★ ----

I dedicate this book to all parents who have experienced the undeserving burdens of nurturing a child with special needs. I understand it takes patience and grace to perform at your best for your child. Yes, it's hard but it is well worth the fight. I know you see your child demonstrating learning differently from their peers which is not an easy task. My prayer is for every individual who knows someone with a mental, emotional, and physical disability will use the power of faith. God who is omniscient equipped us all to have dominion over sickness, diseases, and disabilities. The word of God states *"This sickness will not end in death; but for the glory and honor of God, so that the Son of God may be glorified by it."* (John 11:4). I want to encourage you that God works in the ministry of healing and deliverance through miracles, signs, and wonders. I pray this revelation given from the Holy Spirit will help you develop an understanding that God is faithful and He is able to do exceedingly and abundantly more than you can ask or think according to the influence that works in you (Ephesians 3:20). God wants to use you to support your child to live a victorious and healthy life by taking back what was taken from you by Satan using the word of truth with faith. Faith comes from hearing the bible, and the bible is heard through the word about Christ (Romans 10:17)

Introduction

On July 26, 2010, we had a healthy baby boy with no complications. I was able to breastfeed him with ease. My lactation coach mentioned she noticed a string under our son's tongue, which she explained he might have difficulty in speaking. Our son was such a quiet baby. I had already given birth to a beautiful baby girl, so overall I had wonderful pregnancies. Motherhood has become my new norm. My husband and I were excited about growing our family. I was blessed to have a supportive husband who spoiled me during my pregnancies. All my doctor's visits with my Obstetrician were always given positive reports. No previous recurrent infectious disease or complications with any of my pregnancies. Both children were full-term babies. Both of our children's weight and growth progressed nicely. I felt honored to have given birth to two beautiful

It's Not Your Fault

children.

Our son was hitting every milestone and showing promise of learning new things up until about six months. I noticed he kept his hand balled up in a fist. He wasn't cooing much, but when he was able to formulate words he said mama, dada, eat to list a few with lucidity. He started walking without support on his first birthday during his Toy Story-themed birthday party. I had no complaints, I understood developmental growth takes time; it's a process. Everything seemed to be going well for the Cherry family.

I became concerned as our son got further into his toddler years. After seeking medical professionals and enduring the hiatus period of getting medical support. Our son was diagnosed on the spectrum in correlation with Autism/Asperger disorder at the age of five years old. Autism (spectrum) is a neurological abnormality in the brain which affects developmental growth.

People over the years have asked me how I found peace in God for my son's diagnosis. My reply was and will always be with God's help. I believe I serve a God who can do the impossible and

Rachelle Cherry

He will give me what I can bear. I didn't always have this mentality. It was years of transparency, humility, humbleness, vulnerability, and praying in faith for God's help.

This book was written as an easy read using biblical scriptures to aid, motivate, and encourage parents with guidance and understanding about how to better assist their child's differences and uniqueness. This can sometimes leave the parent mentally, emotionally, and physically drained from the day-to-day hustle and bustle of raising children. I've learned in the past ten years from personal experiences, faith opens doors for the impossible. These faith-based spiritual confessions and prayers throughout this book with physical application with faith will help produce the greater version of yourself and your child.

This book is intended to help you recognize God's plan for your life and your child's life according to Jeremiah 29:11 "For I know the plans *and* thoughts that I have for you, says the Lord, "plans for peace *and* well-being and not for disaster, to give you hope and a future." I found my refuge in God when it seemed as if all hope was lost. People

It's Not Your Fault

may stare when you are in public places. In all honesty, they just want to understand. The false guilt and overwhelming burdens weren't intended for you to carry alone. In reality, unfavorable things have happened to us all and God never intended for us to do it alone. I was reminded that I have a Savior who wants to go through everything with me. I desire to encourage you that your experiences are not in vain. As a community of faith based individuals, we can make a difference and change the world's perceptions of children who need special care.

Denial & Depression

--- ★ ★ ★ ---

"Denial contradicts purpose".

I still remember a moment that happened in the grocery store. I had gone down the candy aisle and I accidentally passed up my son's favorite candy, skittles. I didn't realize he noticed the skittles because I was in a rush. He kept pointing his finger in the direction behind me, but verbally no words were coming out of his mouth. I proceeded to walk, but he started to make unusual sounds with his mouth that I couldn't translate. He became irate and frustrated while crying uncontrollably. It was embarrassing for me because he was making a scene and we had an audience of spectators looking like they could have done better at resolving my son's dilemma. Some stared with judgmental eyes while others were concerned. The "grocery store incident" was common and I got depressed about going out to public places. I was stressed at home because communication with our son didn't exist anymore; not even a little. Even when I made eye contact or when I spoke to him.

As a stay-at-home mom, I created teachable moments with the kids. I loved to work with them together, so they could learn from one another. I even read a book nightly to help build vocabulary, used visual aids for better understanding, and sent our son to school early at the age of three years old to begin the Head Start program, but nothing seemed to work for us. I didn't understand why? Out of desperation, I was completely transparent of my fears when I prayed to God. I gave God my brokenness and I shed many tears.

Since I didn't acknowledge the obvious with my son. I continued to go down the road of denial and ran into refusal. I refused to accept that something different was going on with my son because it hurt too much to face the truth at that moment. I already had a daughter who was learning at a faster pace although she showed struggles, it wasn't the same. I couldn't understand why my son was developing at a slower pace while I felt more confident during my second pregnancy. I felt like a pro. I had refused to see that my son was grabbing his dad and my hands when he wanted something to eat or to get something for him to use.

We didn't realize how much he wasn't using words to ask for the things he wanted because he was able to point it out and we were proud parents.

One uncontrollable day during the children's learning time changed the way I sought and trust God. I ran into my bedroom and fell onto the floor and began to pray this prayer "Lord, help me and teach me how to help my children. I'm tired, frustrated, angry and I don't want to be in denial anymore ….nothing seems to work. I'm frustrated and I need patience because I can't take this anymore. Please help me, Lord." In Jesus' name, Amen. Afterward, I felt a release and I got up from my prostrated position. I immediately went to clean myself up. I washed my face and dried it off. I didn't want the kids to notice that I was sad. Little did I know, that day would change my life. I want you to know the process is necessary, so here are three steps to walk out the process. First, take action in faith. Next, trust the process. Then, trust God no matter what the situation looks like and have unmovable faith.

"Faith is the confidence in what we hope will actually happen. It gives us assurance about things that we cannot see" (Hebrew 11:1 NLT). Faith that can withstand the storms of life. "Take action in your faith because faith by itself it's not enough. Unless it produces good deeds it is dead and useless" (James 2:17 NLT). I noticed different forms of weaknesses such as the inability to focus and verbally communicate with our son. Our daughter's weaknesses were never diagnosed. Even though I had sought out professional help. Our son showed developmental delay verbally, socially and mentally which led to his diagnosis. He was diagnosed with Autism Spectrum. I never defined him by the diagnosis, but I did treat him a little differently. I was fearful of the unknown. I encouraged myself in the word of God. "God has not given us a spirit of fear and timidity, but of power, love and of a sound mind" (2 Timothy 1:7 NKJV). Fear will cancel faith, so stand on your faith and watch God do it for you. "Have faith in God and really believe whatever you ask of Him will happen without doubt and unbelief in your heart". "I'll tell you this, you can pray for anything and if you believe that you receive it; it will be yours" (Mark 11: 24 NLT).

I remember when my son was one year old but he had a limp when he walked. I prayed that his walk would straighten up and the following day I saw a difference in my son's walk. My daughter was four years old and talked a lot but her words were unclear. I would have to translate what she was saying. But one fateful day, I decided to declare that my daughter would speak clearly. Over time, my daughter began speaking with clarity. My son at the age of two started to lose his speech. I asked God to allow my son to say mama and dada. In a year's time, my son lost all his words except for mama and dada. God blessed me by the proportion of my faith. Whatever you do, trust the process it will all work together for your good. I continue to pray daily for God's help and guidance with raising my children. It wasn't easy. In fact, things around the house got harder. My daughter was learning how to read and write but her speech was unclear. My son was struggling with using his words and developing his motor skills. I would just run into my bedroom and curl up in the corner and cry. I felt like crying was my new best friend. I didn't want to face these problems by myself because I was afraid of the unknown. It wasn't long after carrying on this cycle I became depressed. I was so depressed that isolation was my new way of living. I would stay cooped up in the house all day with the kids. The only people I spoke to were the kids. I felt I was losing my mind and the only ones who understood me were my children. Challenges may come more often than you expect without explanation. However, I got a revelation on how to walk out of faith with work. Confessing your fears, confronting the problem, and committing to the process will help walk out faith with work for your loved ones. The ability to confront issues is complicated when denial is the barrier. You may ask yourself "What did I do wrong?" "How could this happen to me?" and most importantly "Why me? Am I a bad person?" Does any of this sound familiar? This is the state of denial. The inability to face the reality of what happens, and mentally unable to address the inevitable problem(s). Denial is your worst enemy. It will have you refusing to accept the truth. You can have all the evidence and facts in front of you and it's still hard to grasp the reality. We all have experienced receiving bad news at some point that would require some type of change mentally, physically, emotionally and even spiritually. Honestly, denial is an emotion one usually feels after receiving unforeseen news. I remember taking my son to his Pediatrician about his delay in speech and developmental growth. The first three years of his life doctors recommended we give him some time to show more growth and development, but I knew something was different. He wasn't keeping eye contact, was easily distracted, unable to identify danger, and sensitive to senses (touch, sight, smell, sound, and taste). His appetite was very particular. Initially, vegetables and fruits were a no-go. I had to visit a nutritionist to discuss dietary options to ensure our son stays healthy.

A parent's main objective is to nurture and protect their child. No one anticipates hearing the rundown of what your child "can't" do. On the other hand, our daughter was sent to school and she started to blossom with her speech. She began to talk clearer and reading was her new favorite hobby. However, my son was entering a world with a stigma attached to his identity. I began to worry even more and my anxiety was through the roof. How was my son going to develop? However, I found peace in praying to God about my troubles.

When our son started to show symptoms of Autism I was afraid. I didn't want to accept he would have a neurological disorder and I believe by faith I didn't have to accept the diagnosis. I just had to acknowledge that something was different with our child's developmental process. I had to acknowledge that it's okay to seek out help so I would know what is happening with our son.

Doctors kept telling me "give him some time, he'll come around". "Boys take longer to develop than girls". I took the advice for my son from health professionals after months of visiting doctors for a specialist referral. After getting no clear answer, I did some more research online and came across an organization that helps children with similar symptoms as my child had. I called the organization only to get turned down because my son did not meet the age group. I continued to call other organizations for assistance, but after being asked the ultimate question "What is his diagnosis?" My reply was always that he hasn't been diagnosed yet. I will always get the reply that unless he was diagnosed, no help was available. I was denied any additional services.

My husband and I had our son attend an in-house daycare in hopes of exposure to children other than his sister to inspire developmental growth. My son at that time was 2 years old and he only spoke a few words, so explaining his day at daycare was difficult. A couple of the ladies from the daycare also noticed the challenges my son had succumbed to and suggested that I scheduled another evaluation. I immediately scheduled another doctor's appointment when my son was 2 years old to get a referral for a specialist. I was more determined than ever to get answers because now his conditions were becoming more visible and noticeable. I discovered in my research a local institute which provided psychological testing and evaluation. However, it was a long waiting list that would take us 2

1/2 years to receive any assistance.

I felt alone and burdened with the unknown possibilities of what will happen next. How am I supposed to help my child, if I don't know what is going on? How long will he be like this? What does all of this mean for him as he becomes an adult? The questions came daily as my thoughts raced in my head for answers. Every morning for weeks I got up only to start crying because of the unfamiliar challenges that were ahead.

I began to look up my child's symptoms online to get clarity. I pulled up an article on Asperger's and Autism that identified individuals who displayed these listed behaviors, which highlights only a portion of the spectrum.

My child experienced these symptoms during the 6-12 months.

- Flapping and flailing of the hands
- A decrease in eye contact
- Decrease of verbal speech
- Lack of facial expressions
- A decrease in developmental milestones (fine and gross

motor skills)

- Delayed cognitive skills

Autism is a diagnosis that must be evaluated by psychiatrists and medical professionals. The symptoms of Autism are a wide range of conditions such as repetitive behaviors, delayed language, and sensitivity to lights/sounds.

I realized the more I researched what I noticed about our child the calmer I became because I was getting some kind of explanation. I begin to take detailed notes of everything my child did on a daily basis. I also noticed what he did around other children. I knew I had to be honest and not in denial about what I saw. I began to take documentation monthly which stated the month, date, and year including shorthand notes on our son's strengths and weaknesses based on his current age. At the age of 3, I didn't hesitate to send our son to school in a head start program even though he wasn't considered verbal. The only words he kept were mom and dad without prompting, this alone happened through prayers when my son was almost a year old and his vocabulary was gradually decreasing. Each time, I noticed a decline in his speech and development. I scheduled a doctor's visit again within weeks to check his health. The doctor stated to me that language takes time to develop, so have a little patience. He will come around. My son would be asked to say "hi" or wave goodbye on cue and our son would do what was asked of him and the doctor would conclude that he was fine. It seemed as if I was lying about my child's conditions.

I figured putting him in a head start program will expose him to other talking children and he will be able to learn from the other children. To no avail, I realized my son needed more support and a smaller setting. I wasn't afraid that the setting was called Special Education. I knew my child worked at a different pace and his development showed some delay. I immediately signed him up for school in hopes that he will be talking and interacting more with others. I brought my documentation of what I observed of my son with me to school for Special Education services. The school recommended an evaluation for a special education setting. He had to get his hearing and eyes checked. Afterward, he received an evaluation of social cues, picture recognition, motor skills, and gross skills. Once the evaluation was over, the school Occupation and Speech therapist stated to me that my son showed significant delay. They began to ask me what he was diagnosed with and I said nothing. I handed over my journal for paperwork. They told me usually a child needs to have medical proof of diagnosis to be in Special Education. I began to cry telling them my journey of getting him help, but I was waiting for a response. A few days later after his evaluation with the school, I met with the head director and coordinator over Special Education.

She was impressed with the details of my notes on my son. She mentioned that she has never met a parent who wrote so much on their child. She also gave me the good news that the personal documentation gave them enough information to help our son and since he had no diagnosis he would be labeled as significantly delayed. This was the very moment that I overcame denial and depression. My son was going to school at 3 years old getting the extra help he needed. I was finally getting some type of assistance.

I was encouraged by the words of God according to *James*

Rachelle Cherry

1:2-4 My brethren, count it all joy when you fall into various trials, knowing that the testing of your faith produces patience. But let patience have its perfect work, that you may be perfect and complete, lacking nothing. The doctor scheduled an evaluation with a specialist for a diagnosis when my son was five years old. Emotions were high and my truth for my child living a "normal life" had a whole new meaning. A journey that will require stamina, faith, endurance, grace, mercy, and perseverance. Yes, all of these are necessary for the manifestation of miracles, signs, and wonders according to Hebrew 11:1 *"Now faith is the substance of things hoped for, the evidence of things not seen".* I know it's easier said than done; identifying the symptoms gives you leverage over the devil to bind and loose by calling its name, its conditions, and pleading the blood of Jesus as the bible states *"I will give you the keys of the kingdom of heaven; whatever you bind on earth will be bound in heaven, and whatever you loosed on earth will be loose in heaven."* Matthew 16:19 (NIV). No, you are not crazy, and knowing what you are dealing with gives you an upper hand in addressing much-needed changes.

It's Not Your Fault

In this continuous journey, you will go through withdrawal from people you know and sometimes those close to you. Withdrawal will make you feel like you are by yourself. You will start to think no one understands what it's like to have a child who requires extra support and attention; how exhausting it can be trying to maintain a working lifestyle, but no one to keep your child who is non-verbal or who struggles with staying focused. Even some family members hesitated to assist because they didn't want to do the wrong thing. I inquired about outside services, but was told my child has to have a supplemental health plan because services can be expensive. I begin to feel helpless and useless to the point of isolating myself from my family and the world. No consistent support from childcare services because my child made random sounds instead of using actual words that people could understand. Each day I felt more and more insecure because I couldn't explain what I didn't understand. Like why my child likes to jump when it's time to sit down or why my child can't handle certain texture items. You can see the facial expressions when you try to explain to people about your child's challenges. Some facial expressions are empathetic and others are insensitive. Either way, you can find yourself surrounded by people who don't know how to help you and you don't know how to confront the situation head-on.

If you don't practice faith and walk it out. You will go into a state of depression. In my moments of depression about my son's diagnosis was the false perception of not knowing what I can do to help him succeed. I haven't even tried to help before I was weighed down with undeserving guilt. It was nothing I could have done or done to prevent his condition. I was fearful of the unknown circumstances of his health. I prayed to God for the guidance of the unknown because I was afraid of not being good enough. I just didn't want to be deemed as a failure. Depression would lead you to a place of isolation and that's never a good thing. You will be feeling like everybody is talking about you and thinking you are a bad parent; when they don't even know you. I know it sounds cliche, but thinking positively while caring for a loved one who has physical, emotional, or mental limitations will keep you as a pillar of strength for him or her during their weak moments. *Finally, brothers and sisters, whatever is true, whatever is noble, whatever is right, whatever is pure, whatever is lovely, whatever is admirable—if anything is excellent or praiseworthy—think about such things* Philippians 4:8. This scripture works as a guide to remind you that it's okay to think about good things. Of course, we all have weak moments and we can benefit from a helping hand every now and then. Depression will cause you to avoid asking or searching for help. I remember hearing a professional stating my son may not ever talk. I must have had a look on my face of disapproval because she retracted her statement by saying it may be different for my son. I immediately put into action partnering with my son's teachers to teach him sign language. He learned the basic signs more, eat, drink, and poop. However, my son had started refusing to learn sign language. I looked at him one day and asked him do you want to use your words?" He responded with a smile. This was the moment that I began to profess that he would speak and use his own words. I do this daily to keep my faith strong and steady. The Holy Spirit led me to some scriptures to support my decree and declaration over my son. *And looking up to heaven, he sighed, and saith unto him, Ephphatha, that is, be opened. And straightway his ears were opened, and the string of his tongue was loose, and he spoke plainly (Mark 7:34- 35 KJV).* I still use this scripture to this day. My son is currently 11 years old and he continues to speak more words clearly. I know some would think why do you still do it? You have to stay in the word of God to keep the faith. *So then faith comes by hearing and hearing by the word of God (*Romans 10:17 (NKJV). I understand everything in life comes with a process. Faith requires work and believing throughout the process. Do not be deceived, your faith will be tested, so putting your faith into action is necessary.

In today's society, disability or special needs are the common terms to describe abnormal or different. As parents we hope for our children to have good health and all their limbs. However, for some of us, our blessing was re-packaged into something special with a greater purpose.

I still have conversations with my son daily because I believe that one day we will have a full conversation together. We will talk about everything and anything. I have faith that I will understand his feelings and thoughts on a specific matter. I've experienced signs and wonders of our son showing emotions of sadness, happiness, and excitement over the years. I can remember him showing a blank stare while I was crying or he would laugh when I was serious. Don't let those moments discourage you. You should interact with your child in a way that makes you comfortable and happy. Make sure you always practice safety so your child will be successful in everything.

I love to play fun interactive games and phonics games to encourage word building and reading skills. These are some of the work I applied with faith to encourage my son to speak more and do more socially with others. Don't set yourself up for failure thinking it will happen overnight because anything great takes time. The moment you doubt depression will creep in to sit on you.

In three practical steps you can overcome denial and seize the moment to make a difference in your community; even better impact the world. First, in all your getting; get an understanding as it was written *"I will give you the keys of the kingdom of heaven; whatever you bind on earth will be bound in heaven"*, and *"whatever you loose on earth will be loosed in heaven." Matthew 16:19.* Reading up on symptoms and early signs of a particular diagnosis will give you a peace of mind as to what to expect.

Second, it will create an opportunity to confront the problem. You can't confront what you don't recognize. Daily confessions of the word of God over your life, your child's life, and a strong support system will help create a positive environment for miracles, signs, and wonders. A positive mindset is the best method of defeating negative and poisonous thoughts. Third, ask yourself; who will you believe? Faith is a process of believing in what you haven't seen and working toward what you want to see manifested in your life. The key is do not waver in your faith for what you are believing God to do in your life.

As a parent who has a child with special needs, you will experience great discomfort physically and mentally. Being overwhelmed with caring for your child who deals with a form of limitation making day to day routine unbearable. I can recall the time I placed my son in his high chair to eat. As I prepared his meal and handed his eating utensil, I noticed his hand was balled up into a tight fist. His fingers looked fringed together as if he had no mobility, no dexterity, or no functionality. His hand looked like a nub, but with my faith I got closer to my son's high chair and grabbed his hand. I pried his hand open and placed a spoon in the middle of his hand while taking each finger to wrap around the spoon handle until he had a tight grip of the spoon. Then, I began speaking to his fingers and commanding it to open and close repeatedly. Then, I put my hand over his gripped hand and showed him how to use the spoon. I took every moment helping him scoop up the food from his bowl while guiding the spoon back to his mouth. I made this my daily practice until I saw him make more use of his fingers and his hands. Some may think that was unnecessary, but when you have a child who struggles with neurological problems you have to consider it all. Some of the extra efforts might make you feel extremely exhausted and even make you feel like giving up, but whatever you do, never give up. Go before the Lord of grace and say this prayer in a quiet place. We all need help and know your help comes from the Lord.

Lord, I repent for not trusting you with (fill in the blank with a specific problem(s) and I need your help to acknowledge what is in front of me. Give me knowledge of how to handle and care for (fill in the blank with name(s) to manifest growth and development. Thank you, Lord, for grace and mercy throughout this process in Jesus' name amen.

Fear

— ★ ★ ★ —

Fear cripples the mind, body and soul from fully manifesting in God's will for our lives. When trauma shows its ugly face, sometimes it's hard to walk in faith. You have to make a conscious decision that fear will no longer resign in you. Fear stops the momentum of faith and works. As parents, it is our purpose to train up our children in God, so the plans of God will manifest in their lives. Don't lose hope; you can overcome fear by praying and making prophetic confessions with perseverance. Prayer is simply talking to God. This is the moment your relationship with God will flourish. Your relationships with God will develop through prayer, so talking to God about your fears and insecurities will allow God to intervene on your behalf. God can help beyond the spiritual realms and shift your reality. He can orchestrate connections for somebody who specializes in speech therapy or occupational therapy to assist. Whatever you need to help your child grow and develop to become self-sufficient. "Keep on asking, and you will receive what you ask for. Keep on seeking, and you will find. Keep on knocking, and the door will be opened to you" (Matthew 7:7 NLT).

Fear feels like a suffocating feeling of the worst is yet to come. This is the feeling I felt when I got the news of my son's medical diagnosis on the Spectrum. I remember going to the doctor's office asking for professional help. My motherly instinct was telling me that there is something different about my son. He would keep his hands balled up in a little fist, he did very little babbling and stacking blocks was even more difficult after the age of one years old which meant he was demonstrating regression. The feedback was only making me fearful of the unknown for my son's future. I began to ask myself these questions. Will he be able to get a job? Will he be able to drive? Will he be able to live on his own? Does he comprehend what is happening around him daily? Does he understand the emotional and physical expressions of others? These questions were my daily norm of thinking and caused sleepless nights. I felt like I was alone and no one understood what I was going through. My husband tried to encourage me by stating that our son will be fine and everything will be okay. No matter how nice his statement was, fear continued to grow.

After four years researching facilities, and being placed on waiting lists. My son was finally able to get a letter from his Pediatrician to see a specialist, a Psychologist. We were referred to a local Psychologist center in Atlanta, Georgia. Don't allow fear to change your perception about a better outcome. You have the ability to speak things into existence that have not manifested. Although, there will be some hard times and you may even struggle with your perception for change. Don't stop believing because with faith and work nothing is impossible.

Fear is one of the hardest perceptions to overcome because the unknown can be scary. However, when you do not address fear it can lead to frustration and anger. "Trust in the Lord with all your heart; do not depend on your own understanding". "Seek his will in all you do, and he will show you which path to take" (Proverbs 3:5-6 NLT). In reality, no one knows what to expect every day, but when life hands you an opposition you confront it. Don't sit back thinking of ways to fail when you are more than a conqueror through Christ Jesus. There's no doubt about it, fear is everybody's worst enemy.

Raising a child who has specific needs requires focus and grace. A goodwill heart does what is right and a willingness to assist. God's grace is sufficient. No matter what obstacles you are facing, there is always a solution. A practical plan with faith can ensure victory over fear. I remember when I had potty trained my child to use the toilet. I created a restroom schedule displaying time frames of restroom breaks and even a cut off time for beverage intake. Strategies such as these will provide you with a peace of mind. Fear is the accuser, so don't allow fear to destroy your faith. "For God has not given us a spirit of fear and timidity, but of power, love, and self-discipline"(2 Timothy 1:7 NLT). After acknowledging your fear, sometimes you are troubled by frustration. The annoyance of not knowing what you need to do for your child who suffers from developmental delays or restrictions. You will begin to notice you are frustrated with the doctors, family members, strangers, and even yourself. The common statement you may ponder is "I didn't ask for this". No, you right, no one asks for this...you were chosen. "Dear friends, don't be surprised at the fiery trials you are going through, as if something strange were happening to you" 1 Peter 4-12(NLT). The reality is bad things do happen to good people, so don't feed into the frustration. I know these attacks against our children are not just carnal but spiritual too. Combat fear with faith and work.

Lord, I repent for operating in fear. Help me Lord to conquer the fearful thinking of the unknown. Guide and direct my steps to assist (fill in name). Help me to see beyond my doubts and unbelief. Give me the strength to walk out your plan for my life which is not to harm me, but give me a future with an expected end in Jesus name amen.

Frustration

Frustration can either motivate you to do better or discourage you to do even worse. We all can relate to the frustration, especially while working and caring for a child with special needs. You have to make sure priorities and balance are in place. Create a schedule that prioritizes daily routines to help manage unforeseen challenges, which will allow you to live a balanced life. Even though the level of support needed for an individual with special needs varies; at least you will comply with peace of mind. It's important to stay calm and focus. Frustration is a common factor for a parent who is doing their best to meet the needs of their child.

I can remember an instance when our son would take off his shoes as soon as he got to school every day. We would get calls from his teacher that it's a safety hazard for his shoes to be off all day. We were annoyed and irritated. No matter how many times we told him to keep his shoes on. It was more relaxing for him with his shoes off during the day. My husband and I decided to create a shoe sleeve that would keep him from pulling off his shoe. He wore it for one day at school and his teachers were impressed as he didn't take off his shoes. He couldn't take his shoes off and after 24 hours of no success. He stopped taking his shoes off every day as soon as he got to school. In the moment of our frustration, we became creative and innovative at the time our son needed us the most because his safety was at risk.

Don't become irate because the child hasn't reached a particular milestone for their age. Don't compare your child to their sibling(s) or to other children because your child is fearfully and wonderfully made in God's image. Make some time for yourself to regroup and relax before trying to introduce new learning practices to your child with special needs. We all need a break, sometimes it's healthy. Think positive because it's a process you're walking out and frustration that is not addressed leads to anger.

Anger

Anger comes when fear and frustration are not confronted. You will become angry with yourself, others, and even with God. You may wonder how do I help a child who isn't verbal? How long can I protect my child; when I don't know how to help? The good news is God wants to hear your concerns and he wants to hear the hard questions. I speak to God about my troubles as it says in the bible "Are any of you suffering hardships? You should pray. Are any of you happy? You should sing praises" James 5:13 NLT. Don't miss the opportunity to talk to God. Get it all off your chest because He loves you so much. "For this is how God loved the world: He gave his one and only Son, so that everyone who believes in him will not perish but have eternal life" John 3:16 NLT. As I continue to seek God for direction to help my children overcome their weaknesses. I encouraged myself in the Lord Jesus through prayer. I realized God didn't see my situation as humanity did. I didn't have to worry about the annoying looks from strangers when my son was over-stimulated. I didn't have to deal with religious people trying to connect my children's struggles to sinful behaviors. I was a mother who wanted to do what was right for her children.

Anger, unaddressed, is dangerous and actions aligned with anger can get somebody hurt. This is called abuse. Abuse towards children who struggle developmentally, physically, or neurologically happens so often it's alarming and overlooked. They are warning signs before destruction. Don't yell at your child with a disability especially if you are angry. Allow yourself to cool off before redirecting your child. This strategy is effective for any child and its positive discipline. Give yourself time before correcting a child's behavior that may bring harm to themselves or others. I've been frustrated while trying to care for my children, but I never caused them harm. I had the strength and wisdom of God to operate in self-control. Discipline and abuse are not the same things. If caring for your child is too stressful, seek outside help or support. If you have a local church, talk to someone. You don't have to go through the process alone.

Have you ever been so angry that things are not going as planned? How do you plan and still keep the faith? Well, make a plan that matches up to your faith. Do the necessary steps to accomplish what you desire. For instance, if you want to become a great dancer, you will join a renowned dance company to help you strengthen and master your skills for dance. The same applies when you are helping a child learn how to talk, write, and understand social cues. You will have to do practical things that will couple with your hope for improvement and growth. I learned that working with individuals with limited abilities requires structure and consistency. They cooperate better when there is less chaos and change. Keep a schedule that works for your family dynamic.

Every day you have to confront the symptoms of your loved one and stay positive that the impossible is possible. You have to know without a doubt that this is not the conclusion. A positive attitude toward a negative outcome will produce patience which will develop character.

Lord, I repent for acting and responding in frustration and anger. Lord, help me to cope with trials and tribulations that come to make me stronger as well as patience. Thank you, Lord, for your grace and mercy in Jesus' name, amen

Grief & Sorrow

--- ★ ★ ★ ---

I remember looking at my children and noticing they did things a little differently from their peers. This made me really sad. I know how wicked the world is to people who are different and how cruel children are to people who look and act different. I didn't realize that these were my insecurities being exposed. Since praying became my daily bread and I read the Bible anytime I felt discouraged allowed me to get past my sorrow. It wasn't always easy. Some days I would go through a crying spell because I felt overwhelmed with grief.

I remember my daughter at five years old asking me why her brother didn't talk to her and why he didn't play with her. My emotions were all over the place because my daughter was crying. She perceived that her brother didn't like her, so I had to explain that her brother struggled with verbal communication. She wanted to help her brother more because now she had understood that her brother wasn't being mean to her, but learning in a different way. As a mother, it was important to talk with my daughter about her brother's diagnosis and the developmental limitations that came with it. Now she is older and she has been her brother's advocate for seven years.

As a parent who has a child with special needs, feeling deep hurts with daily life functions and responsibilities keep on increasing. The cost to provide the proper care will increase and services will become harder to get for your child. This all seems like a setup for failure, but it's only an opportunity to live out of God's hand. God will put you in the right company of who you need to help you. Trust the process God is with you and He will never leave you alone.

Lord, I repent for hurting alone and not allowing you to comfort me. Help me through my grief and sorrow, so I won't experience deep pain. Lord, you are my refuge and present help in a time of trouble. Thank you, Lord, for I can do all things through Christ who strengthens me in Jesus' name amen.

Acceptance

--- ★ ★ ★ ---

You have to be determined to trust God in the process of miracles, signs, and wonders. No, you don't have to accept the reports of the doctor stating that your child may never talk or be socially aware because that is not the faith you are walking out of. You are walking out what seems impossible. You are walking out of what has not been seen yet. Therefore, your acceptance of who God is and what God can do is vital. Your acknowledgment of the diagnosis and its conditions is important, but you only accept what is believed by faith for your child. Who will you believe?

"Don't allow what people have said stop you from hearing what God is saying"- Pamela T.

Don't allow the devil the accuser to make you doubt the very thing you desire for your child. You must stay the course no matter how unpleasant things seem. Your mind has to be made up and focus on what you believe God to do. Meditate on the words of God that will encourage you in your faith for healing, deliverance, miracles, signs, and wonders. Most importantly, pray and talk to God when you feel overwhelmed. Speak to God when you are unsure. Let God know that you are willing to learn from Him to take better care of your child. You can't view your child as the world will be based on the label of disability. Don't let the stigma of the diagnosis mandate your child's future. *"And do not be conformed to this world, but be transformed by the renewing of your mind, so that you may prove what the will of God is, that which is good and acceptable and perfect" Romans 12:2.* Train your mind regularly to think of good things concerning your child. You have the authority to rule over every unclean and impure spirit that goes against God's will.

I remember feeling the courage to go back into the fight to help my son overcome the adversities he had succumbed to. I was no longer going to sit back. You have to welcome acceptance into your life. It's not always easy because growing pains never feel good. However, it's necessary to go through the process of change and mature enough to become better. I had to accept that my son may show a delay in his speech and cognitive skills. There are some instances where children who are diagnosed with Autism can't speak at all. Health and Educator Professionals told me that my son may not ever speak and that I need to see that as a possibility. They even suggested that he needs to learn another form of communication like sign language or use a technology device that would speak for him when needed. I tried teaching him how to sign words. I would say the word eat as I did the sign language for eating instead my son just says the word "eat". I realized that he would rather use his words verbally and from that moment on I was determined to support him speaking even if it meant him speaking in three-word sentences. I was encouraged and inspired by my son's resilience and perseverance. I had to accept that my son would require extra reinforcement and redirecting when teaching him how to be self-sufficient.

You have to embrace the good with the bad. You have to

It's Not Your Fault

understand that bad things can happen to good people. Understand we were created to learn and grow to help somebody else. This is a life lesson that many people tried to avoid, but it's unavoidable. Life is full of lessons like falling off a bike teaches you how to keep your balance or your experience of a bad relationship reveals your worth and value as a person. As a parent, who has a child that lives with restrictions, limitations, and boundaries because of a health diagnosis. You are already equipped to overcome whatever challenges they may face in life. You will begin to realize this is not more than you can bear but exactly is what you need to push yourself into greatness.

Healing

Your healing will begin once you denounce denial, depression, sorrow, fear, frustration, and anger. Healing happens when you are no longer bound or oppressed by circumstances that are out of your control. This is the moment when your confidence is at its all-time high. In John 9:1-3, As Jesus was walking along, he saw a man who had been blind from birth. "Teacher," his disciples asked him, "why was this man born blind? Was it because of his own sins or his parents' sins?" "It was not because of his sins or his parents' sins," Jesus answered. "This happened so the power of God could be seen in him.

The healing process is important because a parent's mental health and spiritual wellness are essential. **"He heals the brokenhearted and bandages their wounds"** (Psalms 147:3).

It's Not Your Fault

Positive affirmation from the Bible will guide you through your healing process. You have to stand in faith in the word of God until what you say happens. As

you continue to pray, your faith and trust in God will continue to grow. You have been through enough now and the journey you are on has taken some unexpected turns, but don't be discouraged. God is not through with you yet. Take time out to think about all the good things you noticed about your child like the efforts of putting on their clothes or bringing a spoon to their mouth during feeding time. These are proof of progress and your child's progressions will vary from another child, but the objective is to always be positive. A positive attitude helps the healing process become easier day by day. Your child depends on your emotional healthiness to be motivated to keep doing their best. Every effort made by you and the child is like a seed in the ground. God wants to water those seeds and give them an increase. All God wants in return from us to give him the glory and for us to testify of His glory. However, a fight wouldn't be a fight without an adversary. Satan wants to discourage you in your faith by using people in your surroundings or even yourself in moments of frustration, so meditating on scriptures will help you to stay motivated in the matters of God. Balance your emotion when you notice the challenges of your child are causing you to feel like a failure. Don't allow yourself to walk out false failures. It will stunt the growth of your child and all the seeds of faith and works will be of no avail. Keep your faith in what you are expecting God to do for your child.

Meditate on this scripture when mishaps come in like a flood. *"May the God of hope fill you with all joy and peace in believing [through the experience of your faith] that by the power of the Holy Spirit you will abound in hope and overflow with confidence in His promises"* **Romans 15:13 (AMP)**. God has already equipped you with the tools and resources. Your mouth is the tool and your words of faith are the resources. Even, the tangible resources are usually already in your home.

You must declare in faith that your child will use words daily, formulate sentences, and have a full conversation without prompting or cue cards, if you want your child to speak. Your experience is real, but it doesn't define who you are and who you will become. You don't have to go through healing alone; Jesus' desires to be with you every step of the way. He considered this thousands of years ago in his suffering for everybody according to **Isaiah 53:5** *But He was wounded for our transgressions, He was crushed for our wickedness [our sin, our injustice, our wrongdoing]; the punishment [required] for our well-being fell on Him, And by His stripes (wounds) we are healed.*

God wants to heal you and make you whole. Even when it seems like your child's conditions contradict your faith. You must have faith that healing is possible and know that deliverance is real. God can do the impossible if you will allow Him. Position yourself to receive miracles of God by working on your faith. Our spirit was created in God's likeness and His image. We are supposed to respond as Jesus did in the Word of God. Jesus trusted God in everything he did. We have to trust that God knows exactly what we need when we need it. You got to know that God will give you only what you can bear. He has a plan for your life and it is greater than you can even imagine.

You must believe that what you want to happen is possible and don't doubt yourself regardless of what others may think or say.

Spiritually you have to be honest with yourself. Do you believe God can heal you and your child? Do you believe that God can keep you in His perfect peace? Do you believe God can give you the instructions to help you assist your child in every need? If you can't give a clear yes or no to any of these questions, then you must get in a quiet space and begin talking to God (pray) and to ask God to help you with your unbelief.

Ask God to keep you during the growing process of faith. Your spiritual healing is being honest and transparent with God.

You have to think positively about how you want your family to grow from this life experience. You have to keep in mind that mental health is an important part of producing good results. I desired that our son would be able to use more words. Although I watched him losing vocabulary words rapidly from his language. Every time when he was able to learn a word and say it, I gave honor and glory to God. I put my trust in Him that our son will be able to continue to speak and God will make him able to use his mouth to speak. Faith is not seeing but believing in what you have not seen or what has not happened yet. The mind has to be conditioned with faith, so listening to someone giving their testimony on the 700 clubs, or meditating on an audio version of the bible, or attending church service where miracles and testimonies of other believers are shared will inspire you that God is still in the miracle-making business. He is the same God yesterday, today, and forevermore.

You have to make time for yourself as a parent who cares for a child with special needs. It is essential to your health to make time to distress and relax from a long day of assisting your child. If not, you will feel burnt out and you will become more stressed. No one does their best when under stress. You will become irrational to your child and be of no use to your household. Your physical state is important because you are part of the support system for your child. I encouraged my son to move around by doing fun activities with both of my children promoting social interactions. We used to play video games like Just Dance or go outside to do outdoor activity stations for

10-15 minutes. This will help you incorporate things that are exciting and stimulating to boost your energy. Whatever will keep you calm and make you focus on yourself is the best option.

Lord, heal my mind, body, and soul from stress and unforeseen attacks of the enemy. Use my life for your glory. Create in me a clean heart, so I can manifest your will for my life in Jesus' name amen.

Advocacy

A like-minded support group is crucial. I have a faith-based community who supports my belief in healing and deliverance. Although the whole process took time, good things happened along the way. My son was potty trained at three years old before attending pre-school and he was still considered non-verbal. He knew how to feed himself. He learned basic words because I spoke over my son in the faith that he will use words. I worked with him daily to use his words by modeling "I want" statements before he identified what he wanted around the house. I did this faithfully until he eventually said "I want "before requesting his desire. I'm still standing in faith with my son because I was told he may not ever talk. My son is currently 11 years old and he is doing better each and every day. His sister advocates at school for her brother educating her peers about the importance of treating everyone fairly. My daughter struggled with focusing and completing homework took hours. Now she is taking accelerated classes including math which was her weakest subject. I am a witness that God can do the impossible. Keep the faith and know you can't fail. Your story, your voice, and your journey matter. It's important to advocate for what you believe in and be an example. An advocate understands faith without work is dead as it is written *"For as the body without the spirit is dead, so faith without works is dead"* James 2:26 (NKJV). As an advocate, you want to set the platform up for miracles, signs, and wonders so God can be glorified.

As a parent, we are all charged as an advocate for our child. You may have not acknowledged the advocator in you, but it's there and it's equipped. Advocacy starts at home. It's your responsibility to educate your child with special needs and create a strong support system of people who want to know what to expect and how to handle an unprecedented situation. A support system that shares your same values and faith is the key. If you are standing in faith that your child will effectively communicate whether they are non-verbal or verbal, understanding agreement in faith with others is important. *"For where two or three gather in my name, there I am with them." Matthew 18:20 (NIV)* You want people to be in agreement with you. If people think you are insane then politely remove yourself from them until they get on board. The most important part of being an advocate is being fearless. Put some ideas into action for your child that you can wrap your faith around. For instance, if your child is non-verbal then introduce sign language or one-syllable words. I introduced my child to both and he was determined to use his words to communicate even if it was a single word at a time. You must celebrate the small beginnings and praise God for the signs. Wherever your child shows struggle, you have to tackle that mountain by taking practical steps to help your child. You can't expect others to do what you aren't willing to do yourself. Let go and let God be in control of it.

    You have to be resilient for your child. Don't allow challenges and the unknown to distract you from what could be. Keep the faith in knowing that things are going to work out for your good. As an advocate, you will have to stand up for what's right to ensure your child's best. Does this require you to be aggressive and operate in a revolting manner? No, you can make a difference for your child and others by making suggestions and informing others of practical acts to improve development functions for children with special needs. Your support system collaboration in your child's life will help build structure and consistency. Giving up is not an option for you or your child. Therefore, your support system should know and understand the set expectations for your child. For instance, if your child is non-verbal some objectives will be speech therapy, sign language, asking the child to verbally state what they want before receiving what they want, or writing down what they want. It may seem like a waste of time for some who believe their child is not competent enough to understand. Practical steps like this may seem unrealistic or out of reach. However, for a resilient advocate, this is possible if you have faith. Faith without works is dead.

As an advocate, you have to be willing to make a change in your perception, environment, and community. Your perception must change. You can't always expect the worst for a child and become unhappy when things are not working out. The fight is real and it's not just a fleshly battle as it is written **"For we are not fighting against flesh-and-blood enemies, but against evil rulers and authorities of the unseen world, against mighty powers in this dark world, and against evil spirits in the heavenly places"** *Ephesians 6:12 (AMP).*

I have seen and heard people say impolite things out of frustration. When a parent speaks negative words, for example: stop acting stupid. It will only birth out the stupidity in the natural. First of all, how can a statement like that produce a positive outcome? Negativity is always going to produce a negative outcome.

Advocacy requires three essential parts: defend, support, and promote. As a parent of a child, who has been diagnosed or having any disability, we have to be the voice that speaks up when our child is not receiving the proper care. It may seem at times that no one is listening or a dead end. Just don't give up! Defend your child's right to receive fair education, defend your child's right to receive affordable services, and defend your child's right to not be exempted from extracurricular activities at school or recreational.

Rachelle Cherry

Support your child in everything he or she does no matter what. Your child has to know that their support is secured with you. Doing what your child loves to do is an easy way to create and develop a healthy partnership with your child. My child loves to jump, so I jump with him every day; we will even jump up with the music. If your child likes to draw, create artwork together for nice household decor. Support builds confidence in you as the parent and the child. The more confidence my son had, the better he did. Some parents feel helpless because their child does things differently, so they may feel like sending their child away is the best option. However, children are a blessing from God. Although every child is different we can't ignore the blessing that was placed in our life and expect something different. We have to approach it as treating our child the way we would want to be treated. Let your actions speak louder than your words and be light in your child's life because of what we give to our children they share.

Lord, use me to be a vessel for your glory. Help me to be a light in the earth and salt in the land. Teach me Lord your ways so that I will help others. Show me your mercy as I walk out this process that was undeservedly set before me by the enemy. Put a testimony in my mouth so you can arise and your enemies are scattered. Get the glory out of my troubles in Jesus' name amen.

Daily Confessions

- ✓ I do not walk in fear, but in love, power, and a sound mind.
- ✓ I will be strong and courageous.
- ✓ The Lord is with me wherever I go.
- ✓ I will delight myself in the Lord and he will give me my heart and desire.
- ✓ I can do all things through Christ who strengthens me.
- ✓ I will cast my troubles unto the Lord and He will answer me.
- ✓ I will live in the joy and peace of my Lord and Savior.
- ✓ Let no corrupt words come from my mouth.
- ✓ I will trust the Lord.
- ✓ The Lord shall renew my strength.
- ✓ God will get the glory out of my life.
- ✓ All things work together for my good.

It's Not Your Fault

- ✓ I will see the manifestation of my faith in my family.
- ✓ I am not moved by what I see because I am an Overcomer.

www.ingramcontent.com/pod-product-compliance
Lightning Source LLC
Chambersburg PA
CBHW031214090426
42736CB00009B/920